HEAD WIND - OW!

C—mac Dyal

ISBN: 978-1-4669-3544-0 (sc)
ISBN: 978-1-4669-3545-7 (e)

Trafford rev. 05/24/2012

 www.trafford.com

North America & international
toll-free: 1 888 232 4444 (USA & Canada)
phone: 250 383 6864 ♦ fax: 812 355 4082

CONTENTS

This book is for my two sisters, Katherine (Kathie) and Margaret (Margie) and for Jeannie and Linda who all made life better for me.

C-mac Dyal

INTRODUCTION

. . . .

This book is a compilation of short stories which are experiences during my earlier years. Many of these stories include one or both of my sisters plus other colorful relatives and friends, and each account is factually true—none of the accounts are made up.

I have chosen not to use last names but first names or initials for privacy reasons and again, every person mentioned in this book is or was a real human being, not a made up one.

My intent in writing this book is to make my family and friends laugh. I hope they do, and I hope you do as well. Some accounts were not so funny at the time and some are funnier in hind sight. Please enjoy reading them, as I've enjoyed writing them.

C-mac Dyal

WHAT'S IN A NAME?

. . . .

In the days of unlocked doors and windows opened all night, my sister Margie (with a hard G), at about age four or five, always dressed in cowboy boots and hat, pants and a shirt, and always carried her blanket. She walked all over the neighborhood that way and everyone knew who she was. In those safe days no one ever worried.

One afternoon Margie decided to try to find her older sister, Kathie. Margie started out on a trek toward school and walked and walked until she got tired. She just stopped walking and laid down to rest with her blanket. When the adults couldn't find her, a neighbor, Mrs. B got in her car and drove around the neighborhood to look for the child. While driving slowly along a less traveled avenue, she spotted a child with a blanket *lying in the middle of the street*. Mrs. B quickly stopped and picked her up, put her in the car and drove her home. She was safe enough now but people knew not to let her get away again.

We left our front door open or unlocked all the time. Sometimes it was locked at night but usually it was open.

Our next door neighbor never locked her front door; in fact she didn't even have a key!

All of this was done during the era of trustworthiness and innocence. Another neighbor used to keep frozen foods in our basement chest freezer and would, at will, come into the garage and then into the basement and get his food or put something in to keep frozen. Several friends used the freezer and had their "spaces" and if you picked up something that wasn't yours, you put it back where you found it and looked for your goods. It was all very proper and safe. One year there was the top of a wedding cake and the top of a fiftieth wedding anniversary cake in our freezer at the same time, for the same year.

Our mailman, Howard, would come into our front living room and put the mail on our "mail table" without anyone having a second thought. The milkman didn't need to come in. He would just put the bottles of milk in the milk box that sat on our front stoop. The gas and electric meters were in the basement and Mother made sure the basement was unlocked so each could come right in and read his meter. It was a different time.

One afternoon, all the children in the area were talking and gawking and excited because the Good Humor man had a passenger. Pete, the popsicle man, never had a passenger—never! Pete knew everybody's name and which house each of us lived in. And today he had a passenger. A tiny child, with cowboy boots and hat, pants and shirt, and blanket. He knew right where she lived, so when he saw her and thought she was too far away from home, he picked her up and brought her home. It was on his route anyway; no problem. All the other children were so jealous and poor Margie didn't understand her new-found celebrity. But she was safely home now and that was all that mattered.

After all the excitement, one unfamiliar neighbor exclaimed,

"Why do they always call that little boy Margie?"

LITTLE WOMEN

. . . .

My eldest sister, Kathie, always loved to organize or direct things and people since, probably, before I was even born. I can remember several plays she would direct at our house; outside during the summer, inside during the winter. She would get the neighborhood children (mostly girls) involved and assign them parts and direct them to say their lines, enter and exit the stage area, etc. We did *The King and I, The Bird's Christmas Carol,* and other presentations and recitals for the neighbors and family members. Many came to these plays and seemed to enjoy them; at least that's what we were told.

One year she produced *Little Women.* At that time I was just a small child, probably three or four years old. I was not given a part in that play but was held back in the audience. This production was to be done at a neighbor's home and of course the neighbor child was involved in the play, one of the major parts. Wendy, who was Kathie's age, Kathie, Margie, and Julie, who was Margie's age were the main characters.

I took no notice of how long everyone practiced or how often, but the production was finally ready for the "stage." The girls were all doing their absolute best to portray the characters we came to love over the years. Julie was playing the character of Beth, and it was her dying scene. While sitting in the audience watching Julie die, I abruptly jumped up and went onto the stage and said to her,

"Julie, are you sick? I'm the doctor."

Needless to say, that brought the house down.

FIREWORKS

. . . .

Many of us have to think if asked what our first memory is. I assume most of us can remember back to about five years old, some perhaps four. Without an outstanding event, I believe that is normal. But I had an outstanding event that I remember like yesterday, and I was three years and two months old.

In our neighborhood, particularly on our street, every Fourth of July the neighbors would get together, collect up everyone's fireworks, organize them, and two or three of the men would ignite them one by one. This took place down the street on the cul-de-sac (know as "the circle") at the bottom of our hill, and from the center point of the circle. Lawn chairs, blankets, and lemonade stood ready at sundown.

Another tradition we created with the first one was, on the third of July the children would get together, supervised by an adult, and run around with sparklers, light black "snakes," do other minor fireworks, and then be required to put finished fireworks in a pale of water. This was done in a front yard—

not on the circle. It was a good solution for everyone and the neighbors got to know each other much better.

So, on July third, 1953, I went with all the other kids (most of them older) across the street to Mr. M's house (our supervisor for the evening) to join in the fun. I remember standing totally still, holding straight out and away from me a sparkler—watching it "sparkle" as it spit and spat itself down toward my hand before it burned itself out. I happened to notice all the other kids running around and "writing" in the air and making figure eights with their sparklers. It looked so pretty and appealing, and they were all having such fun. The natural thing for me to do was start waving mine as well.

I stood still but began waving and making figure eights, and smiling. It was fun. I don't remember the next few minutes really, but as I waved my sparkler down with my right hand toward my left side, then brought it up and over my head and down again on my right side, the fire caught my nicely starched "pinafore" or dress and . . . . PHEWM . . . . my dress was on fire! Then . . . . . , *I* was burning!

What I remember so vividly was seeing my daddy upside down running toward me from across the street, but he was rolling from side to side. I must have been screaming and being very spastic but I could see him clear as day.

The next clear memory is in the doctor's office getting some sort of balm applied and screaming bloody murder from pain. When it was all over, I had diapers taped on my right leg, right thigh, right hip, right tummy and right chest. The next thing was really great. I was given my first Coca Cola—my very own bottle. I was allowed to drink it straight from the bottle—the whole thing!

After that I remember my mother rocking me on our glider on our back porch, I guess till I fell asleep. I also remember trips to the doctor's office to change the "bandages" which was extremely painful again. I don't remember how often I went or how long it took to heal. After all, I was only three years old! But I did heal and grew up and unbelievably have only one scar. It is on my right thigh and only shows when I've been sunbathing because it turns a different color than the rest of me. I think it looks like the state of Utah only up-side down.

As an adult and many years later I found out the whole story. I have already written most of it with accuracy; however, I did not know for many, many years that my sister, Margie, who shared a bed with me then, went to bed that July third evening believing she would wake up and I'd be dead. I also learned that Mr. M saved my face, my long blond hair, and my life by not allowing me to run home as was my instinct, but instead he threw me on the grass and rolled me with his hands until I was "out;" thus my daddy up-side down and running side to side, as was my perspective. The other thing I learned is that Mr. M burned his hands so badly he was hospitalized for a short time but eventually healed, too. If I knew where he was today, I'd thank him a million times over.

I've never remembered any more about that incident other than my parents sending a contribution to Children's Hospital in Washington, DC and that it was mentioned in the *Washington Post's* pages by a columnist (Bill Gold) who knew my celebrity father and made a note of it. I still have a copy of the article.

Am I blessed or what!?

THE LAW

. . . .

My mother always said, when she needed a higher authority, "It's against the rules." At sixty years of age, I still remember this law as the final word in our household. When our house had the very first television set in the neighborhood, all the kids on the block wanted to come in and watch the few programs on the new phenomenon. All were allowed this privilege if and only if they followed the rules; e.g., no muddy feet and no chewing gum. It was against the rules otherwise, and so if you did not comply, you were not allowed in. Mother never had any trouble with the kids.

This law also applied to the rules of nature for some, and when it was used, it was gospel. No questions asked. Final. This rule helped a girlfriend overcome her fear of swimming at a very early age.

In the 1950's our neighborhood was in a quiet, hidden, away-from-busy-streets location and Dover Road was the last street in from the main thoroughfare. The houses were "Lightbound" houses (the builder's name that my mother always remembered) and very well built for the time, with several different designs. The landscape was beautiful with lots of trees and shrubbery and each house had accommodations for parking at least one car off the street.

The street was only about 300 yards long, claimed the best hill for sledding in the winter, ended in a cul-de-sac circle at the bottom, with an intersecting perpendicular small street to the right. Linda lived in the corner house at the bottom of Dover Road and the perpendicular street, just two houses down from us. She was three years younger than I and was constantly and continually at our house. ("Your house was more fun!") My house consisted of three girls plus Linda so Mother always claimed Linda as her fourth daughter.

The summers in Washington, DC were really hot and humid. The 1950's houses did not possess air conditioning but we did have an attic fan which we honestly believed cooled us significantly. I don't believe it any more. We were absolutely elated when the neighborhood powers-that-be decided to build a swimming pool. My family was a charter member unit. It was at this swimming pool that "THE LAW" prevailed.

As was Mother's habit in the summer, after work she would drive the few blocks over to the pool, swim several laps at her leisure and then sit comfortably on the corner of the shallow end with her legs dangling in the water. She would remove the then-required swimming cap from her dark head of hair and lean back on her hands, soaking in the setting westward evening sunshine. On many occasions Linda and I would accompany her. On one such evening, when I was about seven years old, I had learned to swim with my head under water. Linda, being three years younger, was not so brave and would bounce and hold her breath and get her chin wet (maybe), thinking she was also under water. After several repeats of this heroic act, she began to become frustrated, knowing the truth. She was not under water at all. As my mother protectively watched her fourth daughter, she began to try to coax Linda to go a little further under. Linda just could not manage it.

At about that time one of the lifeguards walked by on his way to relieve the sitting lifeguard. He overheard the coaxing and also heard the fear in the young child's voice. He tried to enhance the idea that there was no real danger, but to no avail. Linda grew more and more upset at her dilemma until my mother became alarmed. Out of her mouth popped THE LAW! "Linda, it's against the rules to drown in this pool." The surprised but somewhat proud lifeguard immediately confirmed THE LAW as stated, and Linda stopped thrashing around, stood a moment in the shallow water in the corner of the pool between the ladder and Mother's feet still dangling in the water, relief dawning in her expression, and slowly pinched her nose, took a breath, and plunged her entire head down under the water.

NOT ALWAYS A FAMILY AFFAIR

. . . .

Thanksgiving at our house was almost never just a family affair. There were many years when Mother would invite neighbors to spend the day and share dinner with us. Our house was small but that made things more fun when there was a house full.

On several occasions we would invite Kathie's friend, Wendy and her family over. Wendy lived a block over and shared a house with her mother and grandmother. Her father was ill and in a nursing home. I never met him. However, Wendy had an uncle, Uncle Dan and he was always included in our Thanksgiving invitations.

Our neighbor across the street had a beautiful yard. Charlie was very proud of his yard and never allowed anyone to walk across it. We were only allowed on the pavement, driveway, or sidewalk. Never the grass! It so happened that Charlie's back yard backed up to Wendy's back yard but we would never consider crossing over at that point. We would always drive or walk around all the streets to get to each other (there was not a connecting street to Dover Road). Charlie had a back fence so we couldn't get through anyway.

On one Thanksgiving Uncle Dan discovered a big hole in Charlie's fence. He decided to chance it and come through the hole bringing his dish of cranberry sauce with him. Wendy, her mother, Janet and her mother Mrs. B decided to drive over. While Dan was negotiating the fence hole, the others arrived ahead of him. We happily welcomed them and took their dinner contributions to the kitchen and sat down to visit while Mother prepared the turkey and dressing. After a while we began to wonder where Uncle Dan was. He was running late and should have been there long ago. As we opened the door to go looking for him, he appeared, a bit disheveled with an empty dish in his hand. He had gotten tangled up in the fence hole and dropped the cranberry sauce all over Charlie's back yard. Without Charlie hearing anything, Uncle Dan escaped to our house and he cleaned up and we had a lovely dinner, without the cranberry sauce.

It was some time later when Uncle Dan was in Wendy's back yard that he thought he would come through again to see us. However, the fence had been repaired.

Funny how some adults turn into children.

There were many other memorable Thanksgiving dinners at our house that included Wendy's family and there was one time we included our mailman, Howard, because he did not have a family and would have been alone. There were mixtures of people at our table, sometimes church friends but usually the person who would be alone for the holiday. We often had our German choir friend and nurse, Edit who became a "regular."

As was our tradition back then, after dinner Kathie would play the piano and Margie would sing to entertain all of us as we sat in the living room to listen. Sometimes we would sing along. The night would end with Christmas carols.

Those are the cherished memories I have of how Thanksgiving was and should be. I will include people like Howard and Edit into my home when cooking Thanksgiving dinner even now. It is a wonderful tradition. I just wish we had Kathie and Margie to entertain us today as we did back then. So most of our Thanksgivings were more than just a family affair. In fact, I can't remember having just our own family at all. There was always someone else and that made it special.

JUNIOR HIGH WAS
A PRESSURE COOKER

. . . .

In the 1960's and 1970's in Bethesda, Maryland where I grew up, our currently called "middle school" was then called "junior high school" and included the seventh, eighth and ninth grades only. Tenth grade was the beginning of high school. So, when I was attending Western Junior High School in the seventh grade, I took a course called "Home Economics." I think it was required. We, as young ladies, learned to be homemakers, cooks, nutritionists, seamstresses, and nurses. Of course it was in theory but we "practiced" at it and did learn a few basic things. My best friend joined the "Future Homemakers of America" and ended up a darn good homemaker.

During the weeks that included cooking, I learned nothing, other than to be sure to wash the bananas before peeling! That I remember because Mrs. S (the teacher) demonstrated how it was done. (True story.) Home economics was my first period class after homeroom so this particular morning I strolled into the classroom and noticed that several pots were already on the stoves and steaming. Since the class time was minimal, the teacher had started the exercises prior to our arrival in order to be able to finish the cooking items by the end of class. (That was my reasoning anyway.) I didn't know what we were cooking that day, and I still don't. But I do remember how curious I was to see, so I popped off one of the tops, only the top didn't "pop" off; only the little knob of the top ended up in my hand. It was hot so I very quickly put it down on the stove.

Mrs. S immediately panicked! She was panicky by nature but today it really became evident. She quickly turned off that stove, gathered everyone together away from that stove, sat us all down away from that stove, and spoke. I particularly remember she was overly made-up with face powder and bright "beauty queen" red lipstick. Her freshly colored dark hair contrasted with her face making the whole picture very vivid.

"Do you know what just happened? Do you know what you just did? Do you know we could have been blown up"? Do you know the entire wing of this school could have been blown up?"

Ratta-tatt-tatt-ratta-tatt-tatt! She sounded like a beebee gun. I couldn't imagine what I had done to cause such agony and distress. I really was dumfounded. (Dumb is more accurate.)

"Do you know what a pressure cooker is? It is just that—a cooker with LOTS of pressure inside. (That meant absolutely nothing to me.) If disturbed, it could have exploded. (Yeah, right.) I mean EX PL O DED! Thank your lucky stars nothing happened! I WANT EVERYONE (now she was talking to the whole class, not just to me) TO REMEMBER THIS IMPORTANT LESSON ABOUT THE PRESSURE COOKER. DO NOT EVER DISTURB IT WHILE IT IS COOKING. DO NOT EVER REMOVE THE TOP OR THE KNOB OF THE TOP FOR ANY REASON AT ALL—EVER—NEVER!!!!" The natural red broke through the face powder.

I think we got the message. I certainly did after that rant and of course now I am scarred for life and have never again even seen a pressure cooker, let alone owned one or used one. This is the first of many "mishaps" in the realm of kitchens and kitcheness for me. Ask my husband.

Another day our cooking class was working on making cakes. The mixes were in the bowls and automatic mixers that mix and turn the bowl by itself, (a new tool at the time), were stirring and whirring around the ingredients and leaving some batter on the inside of the bowl I was using. It needed scraping. I picked up a spoon and stuck it right in there to wipe off the insides of the bowl so the mixture would be even . . . .

The next sound I heard was a sharp, high whirr. The teacher ran over to my station and quickly unplugged my mixer. The whirring stopped, the mixer stopped, the mixing stopped and the class stopped. She decided to gather everyone together once again for another learning experience of what NOT to do. This time no redness showed through her face powder—well, maybe just a little.

"Now Class, this is a good learning example of what not to do while you are using an automatic hand mixer. DO NOT PUT A SPOON IN IT! It will not only stop your mixture, it will ruin the mixer as well. We have to throw out this hand mixer. I'm sorry, dear, (now looking directly at me) but you will have to purchase a new one for this class. I'll send a note home to your mother."

From that experience I learned to use a rubber scraper if necessary to get the excess batter, or turn off the mixer before scraping, or don't use a mixer!

From these "lessons" I got lots of education! I've learned not to cook, not to bake, and ultimately not to be in the kitchen if I could help it. Again, ask my husband.

On another occasion, while in high school, I decided to invite my two older sisters to dinner. I was cooking steaks, baked potatoes, and broccoli. That sounds pretty safe, right?

While carefully seasoning the steaks to broil (I usually bake them) I accidentally flipped one over and down the side of the stove between the wall and stove. I had to use a yard stick to drag it out. I washed it off and began again. No harm done. Baking would kill any germs I missed. Then I put the three potatoes in the oven to bake, then cooked the broccoli on top of the stove. Safe enough.

While eating our meal on the back screened-in porch as was our usual habit in summer, my eldest sister, Kathie, sat and ate quietly, making all the "mmm" sounds of a good-tasting meal while crunching on the potato. My middle sister, Margie, did not hold back and asked,

"How long did you bake these potatoes?"

"About twenty minutes." I was proud with a feeling of accomplishment. However, my skill was lacking. Kathie was so polite, sitting there, chomping on the raw potato, acting like it was caviar, and Margie was so realistic. I don't think my feelings were the least bit hurt but I felt embarrassed. I don't think they came over for dinner again.

Aahh. Learning experiences. We are always learning, even at later ages. I learned then to bake potatoes longer than twenty minutes and not to flip steaks. I turn them over using a fork and I over-bake potatoes now. Ask my husband . . . .

(Oh, I think the broccoli was nice and crunchy, too. That was ok.)

HOUSE-A-FIRE

. . . .

During one Fall season after school hours, Kathie, Margie, and I were all home. Kathie was getting ready for a class at American University that evening and had put a TV dinner in the oven (no microwaves existed at that time) before she had to go off to class. In those days our oven was gas-generated and the pilot light had to be lit prior to any baking or oven use. Even the burners had to be lit by a match if they blew out during cooking. Kathie had lit the pilot light for the oven this particular evening and then settled in the living room to wait for her TV dinner to bake.

It was about 4:00 in the afternoon. Mother was at work but only a few minutes away from the house. Margie was somewhere in the house. I was outside prancing up Dover Road riding my beautiful imaginary palomino mare. All was well.

I suddenly heard what I thought was Kathie's voice calling for me. I listened again and sure enough she was calling me to come home. I thought it was unusual, probably not that important but I steered my mount slowly toward home just the same.

To my utter amazement the quiet atmosphere inside the house I had "ridden" away from only minutes earlier had completely changed to panic and a rushing around feeling. Margie was on the phone giving someone our street address. Kathie was in our small kitchen holding two dirty pots from the sink, her left arm up and over her left shoulder—her right hand holding the other pot as it filled with water running full flow from the spigot. Once full, she threw the water contents of that pot over her left shoulder again and waited for the first one to fill up again. She repeated the odd behavior as I watched this ridiculous pattern for several moments. Had she become one of the "Three Stooges?" Margie was now on the phone with Mother, but only for about three seconds before hanging up. What was happening? To my relief Kathie gave me permission to go out and sit on the front steps but only if I did not go anywhere else.

As I sat out on the front steps of our sidewalk with my friend Debbie who had appeared beside me (she liked to "ride" with me—we rode our "horses" together often), I remember hearing sirens in the distance and thinking, "Wouldn't it be neat if they were coming here?" I never imagined . . . .

During the previous week or so my mother had several conversations with the telephone company about our phone service not being correct or an overcharge or some such thing. This was cause for less cooperation with the operators than normal and today Margie had called them several times as a result of our emergency.

Magically my mother appeared in an unfamiliar car, and in her usual stilettos, ran right passed Debbie and me on the front steps. I was a bit put out by this, got up and turned to follow her when about five seconds later the entire 300 yards of Dover Road were bumper-to-bumper fire engines and firemen. They WERE coming to my house! Now I was concerned.

The story goes that Kathie lit the pilot light, put in her TV dinner, and left the kitchen. When Margie happened to go into the kitchen, she smelled very strong gas and looked into the oven.

"The pilot light isn't on, Kathie," she called to my college-aged sister in the living room around the corner.

"Well, light it," came the impatient, non-thinking reply.

Margie opened the lower drawer of the oven, struck a match, and Ka-boom! The explosion threw her back against the sink and onto the floor. Her eyebrows were singed and the hairline along her forehead where the hair begins growing was singed and her face was flushed with a lovely medium rare pink. She crawled on hands and knees over the threshold of the kitchen around through the dining room and into the living room toward Kathie. Only Kathie knows what went through her own mind when she saw Margie crawling, shaking her head wildly and screaming,

"Kathie, Kathie! Is my hair on fire—is my hair on fire??????"

From her college textbook Kathie peered over the hardback and responded,

"Of course not. What are you doing?" In that short amount of time Kathie couldn't' possibly imagine that any amount of gas escaping from the oven would explode. Obviously, Margie hadn't thought of it either.

When both had come to their senses, they realized—the kitchen . . . .

Do I need to tell you the kitchen was in a blaze of fire, burning the kitchen door curtains and the wood door with smoke billowing everywhere? The refrigerator was white but was growing black—same for the oven. Margie, recovering from torched face, hair, and shock, grabbed the pots in the sink and filled them with water and threw the water back onto the oven and door curtains. Kathie immediately took control and grabbed the pots from Margie and instructed her to call the fire department and then call Mom at work. Margie obeyed without question. Her call to the operator went something like this:

"Give me the fire department at 4709 Dover Road!" and hung up. Getting a hold of Mother seemed more important.

The frantic call mobilized my mother immediately who ordered any one of the men she worked for to grab his car keys and drive her home NOW as she scrambled out the office door to the small parking lot in back. One man obeyed without a sound. (Another testimony to my mother's natural ability to command. It was similar to THE LAW.) I think Mother beat the fire engines by five seconds and later said if she hadn't, she would have gotten out of the car and run over top of all of them to get to us. (Can't you just picture it in her stilettos?)

In the midst of this chaos, our telephone kept ringing and ringing until the irritation got to my mother. She picked up the old black receiver and said,

"I can't talk now—I've got a house full of firemen!"

"That's what I was calling about, Honey, to make sure they got there." My mother thanked her sincerely.

While Debbie and I continued to sit on the front steps throughout these moments, several neighbors began to congregate and ask question. Linda came up and sat with us but not before Mrs. W stopped and asked her if she wanted to come in and lie down! Are you kidding? That's the very last thing Linda wanted to do! Poor Mrs. W was only trying to help however she could. She didn't even know what was going on (duh).

In the end, there was damage but we still had our house and each other, but not the kitchen. We did not have to move to a motel or anything, but cooking was non-existent. I remember firemen being upstairs and opening windows and saying we could still sleep in the house but to let it air out for a long time. We were happy to oblige.

Margie was treated well by a fire marshal who sort of took her under his wing. He parked his official car in our driveway (he arrived before anybody in a huff and hurry and slid right into the narrow driveway without a hitch—like a bronco rider out of the gate, only backwards back into the gate) and then drove her, with Mother, to the hospital for evaluation. By nightfall all was quiet again at 4709. Kathie skipped class and stayed with me. Mom was putting Margie to bed after her treatment for "severe sunburn" and fear. Our kitchen was black and scary looking but cool and quiet now. And my palomino mare was safely in her "barn" chewing hay, sipping water, and sleeping.

HEAD WIND—OW!

. . . .

D o you have a member of your family who is a little crazy? Just a little? Just enough to be normal but enough to make you laugh, scratch your head, or stare? Yet you always love being around him/her, even if it's chaos?

At our first family reunion there were quizzes about family members and most of us could answer the ones about Jeannie:

o   Who is six feet tall but claims only five eleven?
o   Who plays *Winter Wonderland* on the piano any time of year and makes you feel like it <u>is</u> winter?
o   Who wanted to name children using only letters?
o   Who was tied to a tree when a young child so as not to get lost (or run away)?

Jeannie is my first cousin, a year, a month, and a day older than I, and one of my favorite people on earth because she is so much fun. Many summers were spent with Jeannie and her family going to Bible School, going to the beach, going to the World's Fair, going shopping. The summers I spent with Jeannie, she and I would make plans every night for the next day's activities by writing down our plans for the day. The lists went something like this:

- <u>Plans for the Day</u>
- Get Up
- Brush Teeth
- Get Dressed
- Eat Breakfast
- Go Shopping
- Come Home
- Take Nap
- Eat Dinner
- Get Ready for Bed
- Brush Teeth
- Go to Bed.

One day while playing on our grandmother's front porch swing, Jeannie and I made up a song just because we saw a fat lady somewhere. We still sing it together sometimes:

"Tell me, tell me, Fat Lady. Why you're so FATTTT!" (Tons of laughter from the two of us.)

Another day at our grandmother's house we found old lamp shades in the basement, put them on our heads like hats and strutted around outside like open-tailed peacocks. There is always fun with Jeannie.

Another summer Kathie, Margie and I spent a week with Jeannie's family at Rehobeth Beach in Delaware. We rented a top floor A-framed apartment large enough for everyone to sleep, including our grandmother. The view was toward the ocean and the evening breezes were nice cool ones.

It happened to be birthdays of a few of the relatives with us so Jeannie wanted to make a cake and do a little play (skit) for them with me. It had to be a surprise so we had to sneak around a lot. While Jeannie was mixing (by had) the cake batter, some of the birthday girls happened to come in unexpectedly. Jeannie quickly ducked into a closet with the bowl of batter. As several of us chatted and tried to get them to leave again, we suddenly heard a quick and distant "tap tap tap tap, tap tap tap tap." Jeannie was mixing the batter while in the closet! JEANNIE!! The surprise wasn't spoiled and we were able to get the birthday people out of the apartment without suspicion.

While the cake was baking Jeannie and I practiced our skit. It was a little song and dance we did with white Navy hats and Hawaiian leis and a wiggle and a waggle. We called it "The Navy Ma'am, Please." We decided to do the vocals in Spanish because Kathie was a Spanish major and helped teach us the words. Our version went something like this:

"Dios quida de ti, Dios quida de ti. En solo an solo, Dios quida de ti."

It was supposed to mean "God cares for you, God cares for you. In sunshine and sorrow, God cares for you." Anyway, everybody got a big kick out of it, especially Jeannie and me. And do you know it wasn't too long ago that I received, via the mailman, my old white Navy hat . . . just for the memory.

One afternoon while shopping on the boardwalk, Jeannie and I found some fake, over-sized black spiders on strings. We each bought one and began to play with them as we walked back to our towels, chairs and family sitting in the sun. A brilliant idea struck Jeannie as our feet shoveled through the sand:

"Let's hold one of the spiders over somebody lying down facing up with their eyes shut until they open them and see what happens . . . ."

Reactions were mixed, actually. But we got several screams, silent shocks, a couple of jumps, a couple of words (like, "you could give somebody a heart attack!"). Then there was the man with the sunglasses on. He lay there and lay there forever not moving a muscle until we realized his eyes were open the whole time. He was just waiting for us to figure it out. My aunt was pretty mad at us and took the spiders away . . . .

Then there were the fingernails on the ceiling. Every morning Jeannie complained that one of us was scratching our fingernails on the ceiling all night long and she couldn't sleep ALL NIGHT. This complaint was daily but no one took her seriously. So one evening my aunt decided to come into our room to listen after we were asleep. What she discovered was that Jeannie WAS telling the truth except for two details. The scratching was not scratching but teeth grinding, and it was not on the ceiling but in somebody's mouth. We never really figured out who was grinding teeth every night, BUT SOMEBODY WAS!

While at Virginia Beach in Virginia, Margie, Jeannie, our grandmother and I all shared one bedroom. One night we all got to giggling so much my aunt kept calling for us to be quiet. My grandmother began telling her funny old jokes and stories in a whisper so as not to get us in any more trouble, but our howls of laughter got louder and louder. My aunt finally came into the room and angrily promised,

"If you don't be quiet and go to sleep I'm going to separate you!" The three grandchildren had hands over mouths but pointed to our grandmother. One brave soul quietly said to my aunt,

"It's YOUR mother!"

Some other comments during life with Jeannie are:

"Jean, if you don't shut up, I'm gonna stuff something; in your mouth!" That one spoken by her own mother during a road trip.

When my uncle was pulled over by a police officer for speeding, the officer looked back at me and said,

"Tell your daddy not to drive so fast!"

My reply: "He's not my daddy."

"Is Rice-A-Roni really the San Francisco treat?" Jeannie asked of a shopkeeper while shopping in a store in San Francisco.

Ya gotta love it.

One summer Margie and I spent another week with Jeannie's family at the beach where my aunt and uncle had rented a small house. I think it was at Virginia Beach.

After dinner at "home" one evening, we all walked over to the amusement park to go on the rides. We walked passed an outside restaurant where lots of people were leisurely enjoying meals, drinks, conversation and company. In today's twenty-first century, outdoor dining is very common. But in the 1970's it was novel. As Jeannie strolled by, she decided to be funny and lean over to see what was on one of the dinner tables.

WHAM, BANG, BOOM! The outside restaurant wasn't outside at all! Jeannie had almost smashed in the front window with her head! The shock wave caused ALL PATRONS in, out and around the place including all of us to look up in great surprise and straight at Jeannie, while the head shock brought tears to Jeannie's eyes, a quick hand over her forehead and a hasty retreat behind her father. She really hurt herself this time and immediately grew an egg-sized lump (this could explain a lot).

"I just wanted to smell that man's dinner! It looked so good." (Come on, now, Jeannie.)

After some confusion and more laughter (except from a red-faced Jeannie), things calmed down, people went back to their dinners and conversations, we continued on to the amusement park where we all went on rides; I got sick, and my uncle had to carry me back to the house at night's end.

I still can't believe she didn't at least crack the window or draw blood or pass out, and I still laugh out loud when I think about that night. I love you, my Jeannie.

Her husband once said he believed Lucille Ball had a secret daughter no one knew about—and it is Jeannie.

OVERDONE

. . . .

There was a time when I believed my older sister, Kathie, would always be at home with me to take care of me. She was always there for me for as long as I can remember. During her young adult years, she met a man who swept her off her feet with charm and looks and Spanish. While my mother was recovering from a hysterectomy, he took advantage of the time and sat with my mother to ask her if he could marry Kathie. She obliged and they were engaged.

The first thing I remember about the wedding was the dress. Kathie had picked out a dress and had so carefully and caringly put it out of harm's way until that September day, she thought. Unbeknownst to her, my middle sister, Margie and a girlfriend decided to take a closer look. After that they decided take it out of the dress bag to try it on. After that they decided to take pictures of each of them with the dress on out in our back yard. To this day, I don't think Kathie ever knew.

As if that wasn't enough, I had a girlfriend, too, and we decided to follow suit. We carefully opened the dress bag and each tried on the beautiful dress and took pictures. Somehow it didn't seem to be as much fun. I guess it wasn't an original idea.

Anyway, Kathie went on to get married in the dress. The wedding went off without a hitch and they were married on September 5. I suddenly realized my Kathie, my "pal" wouldn't be home any more. She would be living in an apartment with her new husband. My "pal" was gone! But Kathie assured me I could visit and spend the night and she would visit, etc., etc. She was true to her word.

One day she arrived for a visit and told us she was going to have a baby. WOW! That was big news! Our family was so excited. Mother was a first child, Kathie was a first child, and now she would have a first child. That meant Kathie's child would be the first great grand child. Big news! However, Kathie and her husband were moving out of the apartment and into a little house across town. By now I was in high school and so it was ok.

Kathie's due date was in December, some time before Christmas. Christmas came and went. And the snow fell about ten feet that year (1966). Because the hospital was nearer to our house, Kathie decided she should spend a few nights with us until she went into labor. That was fine and fun. But by December twenty ninth we were all getting nervous. When she indicated that it might be time to go to the hospital her husband really took the cake. He not only tried to start a fire in the fireplace forgetting to light it, he packed all the wrong things, forgot to put the suitcase in the car, forgot to put on his shirt, and then forgot Kathie. He came back up the snow-covered and slippery sidewalk and into the house as we roared with laughter, and expressed,

"Look, this baby is overdone and I don't want to take any chances. We are going to the hospital even if it's a little early."

Today, his daughter is over forty years old and we still remember how "overdone" she was on December thirtieth.

THE MIAMI BEACH EXPERIENCE

. . . .

In the spring of 1968 I was a senior in high school while Margie was studying in nursing school in Frederick, Maryland. By the end of May, Margie had finished her exams and was on a break between semesters. At home in Bethesda I was still in classes. Margie was desperate to get away to relax but all her friends were gone or still in school. Mother again could read between the lines and decided that if I took my school books along, she would send the two of us to Miami Beach for a week—just the two of us—two, young, blond girls, for one whole week!

My first time on an airplane I stocked up on and took my Dramamine which calmed my nearly empty stomach and my edgy nerves for the, maybe two-hour flight—it also made me very sleepy, but upon arrival we excitedly checked into the Fountain Bleu Hotel. The excitement and feeling of accomplishment kept me awake now. I can't remember the price for the week but by 1968 standards I know it was expensive. We literally could not wait to get our bathing suits on and get to the beach and ocean. We stayed out all afternoon—ALL afternoon.

While resting and sunbathing, we met a family also staying at the hotel. It was a man, his wife and their daughter, Barbara, who was Margie's age. Barbara had just lost her twin sister so we immediately felt and voiced our sympathies and talked and became beach friends.

It was becoming evening so everyone went in to shower, and go to dinner or turn in for the night. We hoped to see our new friends the next day. Need I say we got some sun? WE GOT SOME SUN! We got so much sun we had to take turns bathing in lotion and Noxema—in the bathtub—both of us. I was reminded of the *I Love Lucy* episode where Lucy fell asleep in the Florida sun, got a hospital-worthy burn, held her arms and legs wide apart, couldn't bend her knees, couldn't turn her head, and couldn't walk up or down stairs. She wore a tweed suit in a Don Loper fashion show anyway in order to win one of his five hundred dollar dresses. We felt and looked like Lucy—without the tweed suit or fashion show. I couldn't even wear underwear without hurting.

Somehow we managed to put loose clothes on but we ate at the hotel restaurant for convenience. Sleeping (or not sleeping) wasn't' fun either. My Dramamine had certainly worn off.

Next day we still had red-hot skin so stayed out of the sun. Just the heat hurt. Even in complete shade, the warmth was painful—like opening a five-hundred degree oven door and the heat envelopes the cook. That miserable. In fact, most of the week was spent out of the sun. What a disappointment! In Florida and couldn't go on the beach. How dumb can one be?

Several days later we felt better and braver so in the evening ventured out and up Collins Avenue to see what was what. At a corner waiting for the light to change a man tried to sell us something. I think it was a boat outing of some sort. When the light turned green, Margie promptly said no thank you and we began walking. He kept talking and she kept no thanking him until he grabbed a handful of my long blond hair to stop us from walking off. Margie's quick action of grabbing my arm to pull me away from him exhibited a rather humorous vision of me going one direction then the other then the other. Back and forth. The salesman finally let go and we hurried across the street. It felt as though I left the handful of hair in his grip.

We ducked into a little gift shop and as girls do, shopped around putting souvenirs in our baskets. We got to talking with the saleslady who, oddly enough, was from Maryland. We felt at home. (Dumb again?) We left the shop feeling more at home and with a neighbor, to boot.

Dinner again at the hotel was the most convenient because we were growing tired. No corner salesman in sight on the return trip but we didn't cross over until we reached the entrance to the hotel. (Collins Avenue is wide!)

On our last full day in Miami Beach we felt well enough to go to the beach for a while. I think I took a school book and tried (really I did) to do some homework. If I remember rightly we were either in the ocean waves or under an umbrella, but we were AT THE BEACH! We may have seen our new family friends a couple of times but I think they were gone on this day.

As we packed up and had our last meal at the hotel dining room, we noticed that no one particularly wanted to wait on us. It took an eternity to get our orders in, another eternity to get the orders out and again to get the bill. As Margie and I talked it over we really couldn't figure why the help wasn't so helpful. We were nice enough and polite to everyone.

DING DING! It dawned on Margie (she was smarter) that we had not paid one single tip to anyone the entire week we had been at the hotel. It never occurred to us. Well, somebody got a pretty good tip that morning, and I mean it made up for all the omissions.

Our plane back to Washington was over-booked so we waited on stand-by. Breakfast eaten and Dramamine taken, Margie told me if there was only one seat left that I should go and she would follow on another flight. NO WAY! I wasn't going anywhere without her. As luck would have it there were two seats open on the flight, but not together. We took them.

Since both of us are prone to motion sickness Dramamine is an absolute must wherever we go. It does work—I don't get airsick, but very sleepy, as I've mentioned. Our seats were miles apart but we could see each other through medicine-induced sleepy eyes because we wore these totally ridiculous hat-scarves on our heads—all the way home. One yellow, one blue. We looked like two blond lobster-birds with a yellow or blue feathered head. EVERYONE knew we belonged together, and not because we look very much like twins. Mother was the sole being who would claim us at the gate . . .

It was a vacation, alright. Maybe not the kind you'd normally think of, but a break anyway. It was forgettable but one we'll never forget. Our Miami Beach experience.

MRS. O

. . . .

In the late 1960's I attended Bethesda-Chevy Chase High School (B-CC). As a sophomore, I was the youngest girl on the majorette squad. In this three-year high school, only juniors and seniors were awarded the honor but I was the exception, because I could twirl a baton and march at the same time, I guess.

It was fun being on the squad and performing in pep rallies and at the football games and wearing the uniform. In one pep rally we were placed too close together to the cheerleaders and my baton slammed into the high-cheering hand of a cheerleader. It hurt her but I think surprise was the bigger issue. She had a bruise and blamed me.

In those days I considered myself a wallflower because I had only a few dates. I was very shy and nervous when it came to that subject so I did not date a whole lot. I did, however, date a senior when I was a junior, and everyone knew we were an item. That was fun until I became too trusting and found out through another guy, whom I turned down, that my boyfriend was cheating. He had a party on a Saturday night, invited all his friends and their dates, and we had a fun time. But I found out he had another party just the night before, on Friday, invited all the same friends with dates and swore them all to secrecy since he had a date as well, but it was not me, myself, nor I. Needless to say, that was the end of that.

I was such a sucker, such a Pollyanna. I felt so stupid and used. I was angry, too. And that's when more stories came out. One story is that a year or so before me, my best friend was asked out to the drive-in movies by my now ex-boyfriend. She thought he may try some moves on her (she was correct, by the way) so she sewed her bra ends together so he couldn't get it off of her. And he tried. She only had to say "no" that one time.

By my senior year I wasn't really interested in anybody that was available. I somehow got introduced to some prep school guys and went out with a couple of them. There was one in particular I was interested in but he wasn't so with me. However, another young man was. We began to date and soon became an item in the realm of prep school people and also in my high school. It wasn't long before we decided to go steady, so we exchanged high school rings. Danny's ring was so big I wore it on a chain around my neck and very proudly so. My ring was so tiny that it didn't fit his pinky finger and he ended up shoving is on his ring finger and there it sat between knuckle one and two for several months (until he lost it). We really became almost inseparable and after my best friend went off and eloped, Danny decided he was going to pick me up one night, drive to Ellicott City (a Baltimore suburb) where we could get married, thus we would elope, too. He was dead serious. I was scared he would really do it. Never happened. But it was a sweet thought.

When Danny was ready to go to college, he decided on Trinity College in Connecticut. That meant he would be pretty far away from Maryland and that we would probably break up. That I did not like at all. In order to prolong the inevitable he wanted his parents to take me along when they flew him up to Connecticut. I understand there was some discussion among them, but he won out in the end and so the four of us trekked to Dulles Airport in Virginia and flew up to Hartford for the day. We got a cab and took Danny to his dorm room with all his things and at the end of the day left him there. That meant I would fly back with his parents by myself.

In those days I had not traveled much especially by plane and especially not with the parents of a boyfriend. In truth, I didn't know them all that well. But I learned a lot about them that day.

I knew Mrs. O had a sense of humor and wit and was a smart and beautiful woman. I knew Mr. O was a smart businessman since he was well-known in the Washington,

DC area as a car dealer with a huge following and big deals. The O's were rich.

One evening Danny and I drove his bench-seat "four-on-the-floor" Chevy Nova to a party. I sat close to him in the middle of the bench seat, he had his right arm around me, he worked the floor pedals and I shifted the gears. It began raining. The party broke up early and people were driving home in the storm. Danny had too many drinks. Being famous for knowing how to drive a manual stick, (and for bringing my own six-pack of Pepsi to every party and drinking them "straight,") I decided I would drive us to his house and get him to bed. His school buddy, Scott, would follow us and then drive me home. It was a good plan and Scott was sober.

During the few minutes we three were at Danny's house getting him settled, his parents, who had been out as well, came home. Scott had followed us and parked his car in the driveway, blocking the O's garage parking space. Mr. O got out and pranced into the house to get an umbrella for his wife when she jumped out of the car, pulled her full-length skirt up and over her head, carried her shoes, and ran into the house! It shocked everyone but she made it and pulled her skirt back down. She had a slip on so it wasn't any big deal. I think it was a smart thing to do. And to think that this rich lady had to resort to doing something like that was hilarious to me. How ironic! After explaining our circumstances, Mrs. O was not upset with us and thanked us instead. Scott and I then left for my house.

As the O's and I left Hartford, we had to stop over in New York and change planes. A terrible storm had come up and lasted for several hours as we waited for our flight to be called. By now it was late and dark and we were tired. Mrs. O suddenly said over a snack in the airport,

"I think we should all buy toothbrushes and get a hotel room and fly back tomorrow."

I again thought how ironic it was that this rich lady who could buy anything in the world she wanted was still subject to the same conditions and calamities the rest of we ordinary people were. She must have suggested the toothbrushes plan three times or so when Mr. O left us for a while. He came back several minutes later and announced he had chartered a plane—for us to fly back—to Dulles—in the storm! I was scared about doing that and as we were about to follow him to the chartered plane, our flight was called. We went commercial, but to Baltimore.

I honestly don't remember the flight back. I took my Dramamine before we realized the flight was delayed so I was pretty zonked by the time we were actually flying, which was a good thing.

Once in Baltimore we then had to find a cab that would take us to Dulles Airport in Virginia where the car was . . . .

At eleven thirty p.m. we three were in a rickety old cab that swayed back and forth as it drove down the dark, non-lit parkway, a country bumpkin with no teeth as our driver, Mrs. O and I in the back seat, and Mr. O up front with the driver trying to make conversation. (What a vision.) We were all so tired of traveling—in this ONE day—but we were now on the last leg because Mr. O had made the decision to go directly home to Bethesda and to get their car at Dulles Airport the following morning.

Suddenly the cab went BOOM and jolted around the parkway in the dark and came to a rest, thankfully, on the right shoulder of the road. It felt like a bumpy ride at the amusement park. We were all stunned for a moment. The bumpkin got out (in the rain) and came back to tell us we had blown a tire. The only choice was to change the flat and put the spare on—on a pitch black road—without flares—in the rain—at midnight! The toothbrushes and hotel idea was still the top wish even though it had been nixed. There we were, these two rich people again having to deal with circumstances we ordinary people have to do all the time. The driver and Mr. O got pretty wet changing that tire (Mr. O had taken off his Cartier sport jacket). We offered to get out of the back seat but the men insisted we stay in it. It was not a safe situation, and Mrs. O made the comment of the decade:

"I knew I should have written that chain letter . . . ."

Irony was running high that twenty four hours!

In the end, we got back to their house by two o'clock a.m. (the cabby was astounded at seeing their mansion) and Mr. O drove me home to my waiting mother whom we called from the airports (long before cell phones were thought of) to keep her updated and unworried. She was grateful, I was dog tired, Mr. O drove away, and Mrs. O really should have written that chain letter!

LA CUCARACHA

．．．．．．．．．．．．．

In the 1980's I was living and working in and around the
Bethesda, Maryland area and had been for several years.
My sister Margie, was living and working in and around the
Albuquerque, New Mexico area and had been for several
years. It was not often that we got to visit.

Over long-distance telephone calls during that time, we
twice decided to take a trip together. One trip we took was
to Cancun, Mexico. But this time, with lots of planning and
arranging and accumulating vacation time, we were able to fly
to Houston, Texas, meet, and fly off together to our chosen
destination of Zihuatanejo, Mexico, on the Pacific Coast. It
took me all of the ten vacation days to learn to pronounce
it: "Zee wat en A ho." Obviously, my Spanish left a lot to be
desired. Margie's was much better so she could communicate
somewhat with the locals. Our Spanish dictionary came in
handy, though.

We had loads of fun, despite the heat and humidity. We'd
met a wonderful young couple from New York, and palled
around with them a few times, "playing" tennis, having

drinks, having dinner, having a crush on him, having dinner again, taking pictures, etc.

Our room was in the "old" part of the hotel, the authentic part, where we could really get a feel for old Mexico—tile floor, old furniture, just old Mexican charm. It was delightful. Some of the tours and sight seeing were fun, too. We did have some English-speaking folks around and could understand things enough to appreciate.

One thing that is a must to avoid when traveling is "Montezuma's revenge," or "the runs." It not only dehydrates you, it makes you so sick that you can't do anything but sleep, if that. It's a baaaadd feeling. In Houston, Margie, being a nurse, had gotten and given me a medication to help avoid this curse. It worked for several days, but by the sixth or seventh day in, I began to feel terrible. Sure enough, it hit me. I thought I had lost my entire insides, including stomach, liver, pancreas, bowels, and hoped it had taken my appendix. I had to force fluids and nibble at bits of food, avoid the sun, and just sleep. I had to die to get better. But I did recover enough to meet our new friends for dinner one night although I had to pick at the food. I had no trouble drinking coca cola.

I remember one of the first evenings Margie and I ate alone. We picked a restaurant, showered, dressed, hailed a cab, and went to a remote area where the so-called famous restaurant was. (It was not Carlos and Charlie's—we did that in Cancun.) There were lots of people already there so we figured it was safe enough. It was the strangest thing, though, that so many people kept watching us and looking at us, especially the young people. We figured it was our blond hair and blue eyes that most locals don't see too often. We decided later that everyone in "Zee-wat-en-A-ho" thought we were rich Americans so we were worth a look.

I also remember being welcomed by the host of the restaurant who spoke a little English. After seating us and serving us, we asked, "Donde el banco, por favor," asking for the restroom. He laughed and laughed and answered in quick Spanish, led us to somewhere outside the door and pointed way off in the very dark distance. Of course our reactions were of some surprise. Did we have to go way off into the night into nowhere to go to the bathroom? Pee in the bushes? In the black of night? In Zihuatanejo? Mexico?

"El banco?" he pointed way out. Then he said, "O, el bano? We had asked where the bank was. He knew we meant the bathroom but was having a little fun with the Americanas.

That taught me a lesson I will never forget—the difference between the words banco and bano. I won't forget that even when I'm senile. (I can hear myself now, telling the nurse, "I need to go to the bano—the bano—you know, I have to tinkle.") Nothing like learning in the actual environment.

We got a cab back to the hotel and felt safer once inside our room. It was a little nervie being out there, in a foreign country, not knowing much of the language, without an interpreter, totally on our own, two, blond, young American girls. Anyway, safely back in our room, we undressed and got ready for bed. Now, Margie and I can laugh and laugh and laugh until we cry, just over silly things like the banco/bano misunderstanding. We can see the real humor in it.

What we couldn't see humor in was the absolutely huge, giant, egads, gigantic cockroach just over our heads in the corner of the ceiling. It was the biggest roach or bug I'd ever seen in my lifetime, probably would never see again, and it was right over top of us as we lay in our twin beds laughing about the bano. It was at least as big as a check book. Literally.

Up we got! Panicky, Margie grabbed the telephone and called the front desk. In English she tried to "splain" the situation. Realizing she could not get the message across, she just said loudly into the receiver, "la cucaracha, la cucaracha!" and gave our room number. I think it was about two o'clock a.m.

As is customary in some foreign countries, an empty-handed, slow-as-molasses person knocked on our door about forty minutes later. He did not look too alarmed or happy. We quickly pointed to the giant roach which hadn't moved, and he stopped, studied it a moment, looked around the room (whatever was he doing?) and picked up one of Margie's shoes . . . .

Climbing up on the twin bed closest to the ceiling roach, he reached waaay up, shoe in hand, and began to bang on the thing until it fell onto our beautiful old Mexican tile floor. He then continued to bash it's head in until it was dead, tossed the shoe back approximately where it had been, and said adios, and left us there . . . . with this dead beast on our floor, not to mention Margie's shoe as the weapon of choice.

We were dumfounded. We could not believe our eyes. Is this how guests were treated here? Was this a cultural thing? Was this just because it was the middle of the night and two stupid, "rich" American blonds were scared of a little thing like a cockroach? We will take some of those questions to our graves.

Left to ourselves, and with grossed out expressions, we proceeded to clean up. I don't remember which one of us got the thing out of the room or which one of us dared pick up Margie's killer shoe, but at three o'clock a.m. we had managed to wash up and get back in bed. We were naturally wide awake and began to giggle, then laugh, then howl about the incident. We tried to quiet ourselves in the dark but one or the other would break out in laughter which was definitely contagious and we'd start again. We just could not control it. I believe we got zero sleep that night and were exhausted from laughing. My stomach was actually sore.

In another day or so we headed out for the airport to go home. We did the reverse of our meeting; flew to Houston, said our good byes and each flew home, one to Albuquerque, the other to Bethesda. The things we will never forget about that trip are, of course, Montezuma's revenge, the darling couple from New York, the beach, the restaurants, the tours, the jewelry we bought, the heat and humidity, our lovely old Mexican room, pronouncing Zihuatanejo, el banco and el bano, laughing till we were sick, and we will NEVER forget that huge, killer cockroach and how the circumstances were handled. It is funny now, but it wasn't then.

Aahhh, memories. Sometimes things are funnier later than they are at the time . . . .

Right, Margie?

THE BONE

. . . .

My Sister, Margie, and I were driving east across the country from New Mexico to Washington, DC. It was my car, a 1974 blue and white firebird (I was so proud of that car). Margie was driving now after trading off with each other all during this long September day. The road was an interstate highway but a two-lane road on our side, with steady traffic to our right, in front and in back, and all of us doing about sixty to sixty-five mph. There was a concrete barrier uncomfortably on our left.

All at one, it was over! We were shocked at having driven over an animal in our lane and no where else to go. Nope, we had to drive right straight over it, if the car could *get* over it. The firebird was built low to the ground. It was a "hot" car at the time. It was my baby. I tell you, so much happened in that one little second. I hoped a car or two in front of us actually killed the thing before we got to it. And what if we lost complete control and veered—in any direction? Would we be hurt or killed? Would we hurt or kill someone else?

Would all our cars be smashed to smithereens? Yet, the car in front of us went over it without a hitch . . .

"What was THAT? Looked like a big dog."

"Maybe a calf or a pig." We settled on a small deer, but there was really no telling.

We kept going with the traffic, watching in the rearview mirrors the cars behind us do the same bump and thump we had just done then realized we were ok. We really were ok. We jumped the thing without a hitch, just as the car in front of us had. No swerving, no veering out of control. It was an Olympic Ten! Miracle of miracles.

We soon settled down again to our plan of looking for a town, place to eat, and a motel for the night. It was an autumn Saturday night, in the middle of the United States, somewhere on Route Forty, dark, and unfamiliar. Just the two of us—young, blond, trusting girls.

It was nearing nine thirty p.m. when we finally came to what looked like a small town that had what we needed. The first order of business was to get gas, then dinner, then a motel. After turning off the ignition, gassing up and getting information, the baby blue would absolutely **not** start. My car was having none of it. It was a "hot" car and it had its own way tonight.

After my several tries at turning the ignition key without success, the attendant got way down there on his hands and knees, almost stomach-on-the-ground, and peered underneath the dark area. In his mid-country-bumpkin drawl, he exclaimed,

"Looks lack a sti-eck got stuck in yer transmission box."

I thought of the *I Love Lucy* episode when the Ricardos and Mertzes drove through Tennessee, stopping at a filling station. After several finger drawings in mid air, back and forth, in and out, over and under, around one way then the other, the attendant's comment was, "Nope, ya cain't git thar." Anyway, in the end, we called a tow truck to come get us and the car, and deliver us to our motel choice.

It took the man every bit of an hour and a half to reach us in this small town at the well-known gas station on this late Saturday night, (we could have walked backwards to the motel if we'd known it was just a few short blocks away before he got there). The company's logo was painted boldly on the sides of the tow truck shouting its name we will never forget: *"S P E E D Y 'S TOWING SERVICE."* (Don't you love irony . . . .)

Our dinner consisted of potato chips, an orange, a Coke and a hot shower and we concluded our evening by going to sleep, deciding to make our plans for Sunday on Sunday morning, when we were a bit more refreshed.

At nine o'clock Sunday morning I did not feel more refreshed. Margie is stronger and began looking through the local telephone book for auto shops that might be open. She called several that did not answer. However, surprisingly, one shop keeper answered the call and instructed us to come right over. We thought victory was imminent.

We again called for a tow truck, joking with each other about "Speedy's" service the night before. We knew this morning would be better.

Glad we didn't bet the farm because forty forevers later, not only was Speedy's Towing Service truck at our motel, it was the same driver. Seeing that same truck and that same driver sorta made you happy and sad at the same time. We were being rescued but we'd be in a nursing home before the car would start.

"How ya girls doin' this mornin'?" he was being pleasant, recognizing us from the night before. He acted as if it was a joke. Guess it was from our standpoint.

He loaded the car up and we got in the front seat again and I suggested that he drive us all the way to DC. He thought that was cute. I thought it was pretty funny. We rode about five minutes to the local superstore's auto department. After a few minutes of fussing around, my baby blue was sitting on a rack in the garage of K-Mart. We paid Speedy and said good bye as he drove off. We felt a bit like hot potatoes being tossed from one person to another, trading the only familiar face for another unfamiliar face and place. Yet it was oddly a relief as well.

Now assessing our situation, we were together; it was daylight; we knew K-Mart stores; the auto department *was* open; and the mechanic was ready to work. Go with it.

After a maximum question and answer period, the young mechanic was ready to have a hands-on look. Nothing unusual under the hood; radiator filled and in tact; oil and other fluids looked good; ignition not engaging and automatic transmission frozen.

"Could be the starter," suggested the mechanic. He made me think of Gomer Pyle from the old *Andy Griffith Show*. He fooled around and fooled around and walked around and scratched his head and finally got on the ground to look underneath.

"Somethin' thar I'd lack to see up close. We'll have to jack 'er up. Which one a ya wants to git in?"

"Get in! What do you mean 'get in'?" Margie has always been more outspoken and less shy. "I certainly don't want to get in while you hoist the car up—how high?"

"'Bout tin feet's all. It's safe enough."

"Right." Margie was also braver. I said nothing, and she opened the driver's door, got in, shut it, but couldn't put down the electric window. The car began to rise slowly.

"Get ready to bury me when this is over." She had a way with words to lighten an otherwise scary situation. "Better put on the seat belt."

As the car slowly ascended, I saw less and less of Margie's head. Gomer walked straight under the car, looked up at its underbelly and shouted over the noise of the mechanical jack,

"Thar's a bone stuck in yer transmission box." You'd've thought we'd won an Oscar. "And thar's furrr stuck all around it, too. Run over any critters?"

Hmmm . . . .

"Yes, we did last night. We couldn't help it. We were in traffic on the interstate." That was my "so sorry, I apologize" voice. I felt bad for the critter.

"Well, he left his rib bone stuck ri-jeer. That may be the whole problem, ladies. I'll jes raise this here car a little higher so's I kin work on it." So up she went even higher—maybe two feet.

I'm sure the ten or fifteen minutes seemed like ten hours to Margie when Gomer finally began calling out orders for her to move the gear shift lever.

"Kin ya git 'er outta park? Ok, now put 'er in reverse; now neutral; now drive, now back to neutral, now reverse, now park. Do it ag-in." Margie was careful to move only her right arm following these instructions so as not to tip the car over and fall "tin" or more feet to certain death.

"Now we'll try with the ingine on. Go ahead when yer ready up thar."

I began to pray. I knew Margie was praying since her feet left the cement.

"No need fer the brake. Jes switch 'er on and move the geer sti-eck lack before, slowly through each geer. Then back ag-in. OK, looks good ta me. I'll bring ya down now."

As the car and my sister slowly descended, I began adding up charges. My travelers' cheques were diminishing with each command and movement. Would we even have enough to pay for this work, and on a Sunday? Oh boy; worry began to take over.

It was now safe for Margie to get out of the car which she couldn't do fast enough.

"Guess I won't have to pay for your funeral," I quipped. She was clearly shaken from this high-in-the-garage sky ride with a young country bumpkin's judgments, analysis, vocal instructions, and workmanship. Not exactly a confident feeling of safety. But her two feet were back on land and she was taking deep breaths.

"If ya two want sum lunch, go on in the store and set awhile and eat. I'll jes clean 'er up a little. Be 'bout twenty to thirty minutes I guess.

Inside the K-Mart and of course on the other end of the building, we found a tiny eating area. I think we got pizza and talked over our expense situation. If we had to, we'd charge the thing and worry about it later. We were already a day late, certainly now a dollar short and tired from the ordeal, especially Margie. It was already after three o'clock p.m. with the sun fading. How far could we really drive from here leaving so late in the day? We decided to go on down the road even if it was twenty miles or fifty miles just to feel like the day wasn't a total waste—that is, if we didn't have to spend the night in jail for insufficient funds.

Back at the garage we waited for the bad news. I just knew it would take most, if not all, of my travelers' cheques plus cash. Margie was counting up her money. We prepared for the worst.

"That'll be twailve dollars and twinty-fi cent, ma'am."

"Beg your pardon. Did you say twelve dollars and twenty-five cents?" I couldn't be sure I heard or understood him correctly.

"That's what I said."

I was about to ask if he'd made a mistake when my sister poked me with her hidden elbow.

"That's really **all** we owe, for everything you did?" Margie sweetly questioned.

Yep. That's it. An thanks fer yer bidness. Hope ya have a safe trip home. Come back and see me some time."

We'd been through thumps and bumps, killed an animal, killed and resurrected a car, waited an eternity for towing service, no dinner, less sleep, more waiting, worry and daring acts of bravery in the past twenty-four hours, but this took the cake. It was a good thing, our shining light. But I truly did not want to come back and see Gomer Pyle again.

He would absolutely **not** take any more than that twelve dollars and twenty-five cents; no tip, no nothing. (How many times did we thank him, Marg?)

And we're off again, driving east on Interstate Forty, in the dusk of evening, somewhere in the middle of the United States. It wasn't ten minutes. The smoke shocked and blinded us. Luckily we were near an exit ramp so pulled off and over. My firebird was burning! Smoke poured out from under the hood. We couldn't see much. We were deflated, and it wasn't the tires.

Oh, we were so disappointed. I popped open the hood and more smoke rushed to escape. What now? As assessed, we were in the middle of the country, alone, at five thirty p.m. on a Sunday night, with a smoking car (unlike a "smokin'" car). Another good Samaritan pulled off the road next to us to take a look. I think the truck driver just felt sorry for us. But we'd take the help.

"It looks like it's just a belt or a clip missing. Nothing major, ladies." Hey, it wasn't Gomer Pyle or Goober! He continued. "There's a filling station right over there across the highway. If you can get 'er there, I think they close at six. Good luck and sorry I couldn't be of more help." And he was gone.

An angel in disguise?

The station attendant looked under the hood, explained that a clip was missing and he had one (it just came in)—it would take only a few minutes, unless we wanted to bring the car back the next day . . . .

Five dollars and thirty minutes later we were again aiming our way for Washington, DC. Our day had been a full one with literally highs, lows, a bone, smoke, a clip, and no mileage to speak of. So we got off at a nearby exit and checked into another motel for the night and looked forward to another day in the adventures of Margie and Carolyn driving home. When we did get home we were a day early with money in our pockets.

Margie telling "the bone story" is really much funnier than what had actually happened. We told that story so many times, to new listeners, the same listeners, and to requests for a repeat performance, that even these many years later, all we have to say is, "the bone story" and people start laughing as if it was the first time they'd heard the long version. How my "smokin' hot car" got through that and stayed with me for several years after is known only to God.